THE ANCIENT RAIN

Also by Bob Kaufman

Golden Sardine (City Lights Books)
Solitudes Crowded with Loneliness

Bob Kaufman
THE ANCIENT RAIN:
Poems 1956~1978

A NEW DIRECTIONS BOOK

Grateful acknowledgment is made to the editors and publishers of the
following journals and magazines in which some of these poems first
appeared: *Bastard Angel, Beatitude, Ins and Outs, Semina,* and
Vanishing Cab.

The first stanza of "Picasso's Balcony" first appeared in Bob Kaufman's
Golden Sardine. (Copyright © 1967 by Bob Kaufman. Reprinted by
permission of City Lights Books.)

Manufactured in the United States of America
First published clothbound and as New Directions Paperbook 514 in 1981
Published simultaneously in Canada by George J. McLeod, Ltd., Toronto

Library of Congress Cataloging in Publication Data

Kaufman, Bob.
  ' ' ' The ancient rain.
    (A New Directions Book)
    Includes index.
    I. Foye, Raymond, 1957–. II. Title.
PS3561.A84A8   811'.54   81-1250
ISBN 0-8112-0790-0   AACR2
ISBN 0-8112-0801-X (pbk.)

New Directions Books are published for James Laughlin
by New Directions Publishing Corporation
80 Eighth Avenue, New York 10011

THE ANCIENT RAIN

EDITOR'S NOTE

"I want to be anonymous," Bob Kaufman said one rainy night in a San Francisco saloon. I had sought out the reclusive and uncommunicative poet for nearly a year before he appeared suddenly in a café and took me by the arm to a deserted Chinatown bar. Alone together, his pronouncements were extreme and final. "I don't know how you get involved with uninvolvement, but I don't want to be involved. My ambition is to be completely forgotten."

For the past two decades Kaufman has been engaged in the active practice of being obscure, living the Orphic myth, adroitly avoiding all public contact. He had been a legendary figure among the jazzmen and bohemians of the nineteen-forties and 'fifties. Flamboyant and quick-witted, he was the original "beatnik"—a word he invented. His three broadsides (*Abomunist Manifesto, Second April, Does the Secret Mind Whisper?*), published by Lawrence Ferlinghetti's City Lights Books, became overnight classics of the Beat Generation. Adapting the harmonic complexities and spontaneous invention of be-bop to poetic euphony and meter, he became the quintessential jazz poet.

So absolute was Kaufman's dedication to the oral and automatic sources of poetry, it was only at the insistence of his wife, Eileen, that he began to write down his work. With one exception, the earliest surviving poem in this volume dates from the night of their first meeting in 1957. Their life in San Francisco's North Beach centered on the Co-existence Bagel Shop, where he held court. Carrying his son Parker in a clarinet case, Kaufman horrified the locals with his unruly antics and soon became the target of beatings and harassment by the city police.

Kaufman left San Francisco for New York in the spring of 1960. He had been invited to read at Harvard University and was to begin work on his first book, *Solitudes Crowded with Loneliness* (New Directions, 1965). But the New York years were filled with poverty, addiction, and imprisonment. "Blood

Fell on the Mountains," composed upon his return to San Francisco in 1963, portrays his sorrow and disillusionment. "Small Memoriam for Myself," written the following week, became a final supplication. Three days later, Kaufman took a ten-year Buddhist vow of silence, prompted by the assassination of President Kennedy. For the next decade he neither spoke nor wrote.

Kaufman broke his silence in February 1973 on the day the Vietnam War ended. He stunned a local gathering one evening by reciting Thomas à Becket's speech from T.S. Eliot's *Murder in the Cathedral* ("They know and do not know, what it is to act or suffer. . . ."), followed by his own untitled poem which begins section two ("All those ships that never sailed . . ."), which, like many of the poems in this volume, has been transcribed from a tape recording.

During the next five years, Kaufman composed some of the finest poems of his career—simple, lofty, and resplendent. In the poem "The Ancient Rain," he renews his preoccupation with Federico García Lorca, as he seeks to reconstruct the battered psyche of the Black man through poetry. In 1978, Kaufman abruptly renounced writing and withdrew once again into silence.

This book comprises the uncollected poems of Bob Kaufman. In the end, it received the poet's blessings. I am indebted to the publishers of Bob Kaufman's poetry through the years, to Neeli Cherkovski, who assisted in tracking down many of these poems, to Fred Martin and Peter Glassgold at New Directions, and most importantly to Eileen Kaufman, without whom this book would not exist. My love and gratitude.

Raymond Foye
27 October 1980
New York City

x

Poems
1956–1963

PRIVATE SADNESS

Sitting here alone, in peace
With my private sadness
Bared of the acquirements
Of the mind's eye
Vision reversed, upended,
Seeing only the holdings
Inside the walls of me,
Feeling the roots that bind me,
To this mere human tree
Thrashing to free myself,
Knowing the success
Of these burstings
Shall be measured
By the fury
Of the fall
To eternal peace
The end of All.

LORCA

   Split ears of morning earth green now,
Love and death twisted in tree arms,
   Come love, throw out your nipple
to the teeth of a passing clown.

Spit olive pits at my Lorca,
Give Harlem's king one spoon,
At four in the never noon.
Scoop out the croaker eyes
   of rose flavored Gypsies
Singing García,
In lost Spain's
Darkened noon.

DEAR PEOPLE

We cut our teeth on oyster shells,
We were suckled on father's milk,
So what?
Broken homes,
Don't cop out,
Buying diamonds
Off the backs of
South African Negroes
The wax bitches
Are well dressed tonight,
Dear people,
Let us
Eat jazz.

[THESE DAYS AND WEEKS]

These days and weeks
That cannot be found on any calendar,
These hours and minutes unknown to the clock,
When all those rusting ships of the past, long gone
To the bottom of life, guarding the sunken dreams
Cast up their sorrows to swell this grief with memory.

Terror is around us both my soul. Nothing else will come.
I cannot describe the horrors, and worse, I cannot flee.
A wall is all.
I am hacked by knives I do not see, stung by stinging bee,
I can only bleed in silence, my pains are numb with admiration.

Where do you keep them all, my soul? How long can you stand?
What question is this being asked, can humans ever know?
Mad teeth are in the forms of man and chew my love to bits,
And I can do nothing, my soul, but wait their clawing cut,
    Asking only that my flesh holds
    & my anguished mind's reassurance in surprise,
    & my love survive these brutal enigmas,
    That I please you, my Soul . . . if only you alone.

AWE

At confident moments, thinking on Death
I tell my soul I am ready and wait
While my mind knows I quake and tremble
At the beautiful Mystery of it.

PICASSO'S BALCONY

Pale morning light, dying in shadows, loving the earth in midday rays, casting blue to skies in rings, sowing powder trails across balconies. Hung in evening to swing gently, on shoulders of time, growing old, yet swallowing events of a thousand nights of dying and loving, all blue. Gone to that tomb, hidden in cubic air, breathing sounds of sorrow.

Crying love rising from the lips of wounded flowers, wailing, sobbing, breathing uneven sounds of sorrow, lying in wells of earth, throbbing, covered with desperate laughter, out of cool angels, spread over night. Dancing blue images, shades of blue pasts, all yesterdays, tomorrows, breaking on pebbled bodies, on sands of blue and coral, spent.

Life lying heaped in mounds, with volcano mouth tops, puckered, open, sucking in atoms of air, sprinkling in atoms of air, coloring space, with flecks of brilliance, opaline glistening, in eyes, in flames.

Blue flames burning, on rusty cliffs, overlooking blue seas, bluish. In sad times, hurt seabirds come to wail in ice white wind, alone, and wail in starlight wells, cold pits of evening, and endings, flinging rounds of flame sheeted balls of jagged bone, eaten, with remains of torn flowers, overwhelming afterthoughts, binding loves, classic pains, casting elongated shadows, of early blue.

Stringing hours together in thin melodic lines, wrapped around the pearl neck of morning, beneath the laughter, of sad sea birds.

RUE MIRO

MIRO . . . THE FLOWERS ARE UP THERE ON THE WALL WHERE I
LAST SAW THEM & THE TIME BEFORE THAT, VARIOUS,
WITH HOT DOTS STICKING OUT ALL OVER, PRANCING
DARKLY IN THEIR WOODEN FRAME, THEIR WALL, DANC-
ING LIKE GYPSIES ON THE ROOF OF A DRUM . . .

MIRO . . . THERE IS A STREET WITH YOUR NAME, NAMED BEFORE
YOU, AFTER YOU, THEN AND NOW IT FLOATS IN DROPS
AND SHADINGS, STRANDED IN A FAKE SPAIN, FARTHER
THAN MONTROICH, WAY OFF,
A WET PLACE, OF HOT RAINS, & YELLOWED LONG LEAF
PLANTS, NAMED FOR A BROKEN SUN KING, LOUISIANA,
RHYMES WITH YESTERDAY, GONE, PAST, MOVED ON,
GHOSTLY, BROWN WISHES . . .

MIRO . . . YOUR NAME IS A BLACK RIBBON IN A STABBED LAND-
SCAPE, RAVED COLD FORMS SLANTED AGAINST A STEW
OF BURNING SYMBOLS & EYES.
BLATANTLY HONKING DUCKS GO UNNOTICED IN EXPENSIVE
FEATHERS, A FACELESS PLACE OF CURVING BLOOD & FIN-
GERING MOTIONS . . .

MIRO . . . EMPTY TURTLES, GLIDE BETWEEN A DIVIDE OF BAROQUE
HOTELS, FLEEING TO SHELLY NEST DEEP INSIDE A SCOOPED
OUT TRUTH, A SCOPE OF THINNING CRIES, A CHORUS OF
GRINNING OYSTERS, HEAVY DRAPERIES FROM TOULON, &
ROOMS OF DROWNING FURNITURE, DANGLING IN THE
MIND'S EYE, A WALK THROUGH THE BERSERK AIR,

MIRO . . . I WAS BORN ON YOUR STREET, FORTY THOUSAND YEARS
AGO IN A YEAR OF APRILS & SCREAMED A FLOCK OF
DAZED GEESE STAGGERED.

MIRO . . . ON THAT STREET, I HEARD A FEVER & SAW A WHITE
MOON, BY THE GALVEZ GREENS, BROKEN INTO MILLIONS
OF TRANSPARENCIES.

INQUIRY INTO A DECEMBER BECAUSE

The descendants of dinosaurs are quicksand men, holy crime
minds, dripping fake myths.

Those germinal wise men circumcised trees, demolished time,
invented mushrooms, those rubber toes of God.

I am being followed by hot butterflies and pickpockets have
lifted my navel. Stony crows have wakened me cawing at the
moon.
My eye leaks, dripping sight all over my collar.

Fake mystics, who photograph
God, while ecstatic pygmies
Burped the Christ child,
Murmuring, smile, baby,
It's your birthday.

COUNTESS ERICA BLAISE: CHORUS

Erica Blaise began life with several established truths in her mouth, one was that her father owned three governments and held options on two more. The other was that she was ugly; the aesthetics of her physical make-up had been poorly handled by her maker, and as though in remorse, he had endowed her with all the appetites he had not lavished on the Marquis de Sade. It would not do to bore one with the education and girlhood of an aristocratic European girl, as their lives do not begin until all that is done with, stored with bloomers. Erica, being Countess Blaise, was not allowed to destroy ordinary people, that is, people whose annihilation is handled on a corporate scale. This placed her in the uncomfortable position of having to find two people who were not already spoken for, which is no small task today. Of course, after poking around the flabby corners of humanity, she discovered that the only group still available and in plentiful supply were artists; what's more, they seemed to enjoy it, even demanding wounds that no one was prepared to inflict, as though their diet was pain— flavored with self-taught self-pity. Erica would not let such hungry people starve, for that would not be civilized. Neither would she turn her back on any who seemed worthy of such historical attentions. She began by collecting major works by artists whose triumphs had placed them outside her game preserve, unearned trophies, but useful lures for less wily game stalking the well-framed jungle. Indiscriminate in her choice of charms to dangle from her social bracelet, she concocted a hodgepodge of self-immolators, unique only for its variety, angelic American girl refugees from Nebraska Victorianism, grateful for the chance to buy Sorbonne dreams in her richly lavendered armpits, English prose writers fleeing Berlitz concentration camps, New York painters pining for one-man shows, which she allowed them to put on so long as they didn't hang pictures, stone cutters, pastel chewers, wire benders, Arab boys with mosaic buttocks, inventors of new artistic movements that lasted one week, unless they became exhausted before the week was out—and fled to Marseilles. Blond German Faustian youth swearing to paint Nietzsche while tripping over borrowed evening gowns amid superman Teutonic giggles, hot-blooded Spaniards who had to be reheated every hour, who painted only their lips, sexy South Americans who slept in boots, and only with each other, explosive Mexicans who would paint only mountains and made love to kill time, Andalusian Gypsies with Flamenco dripping from their fingertips, who would not sin in the same room with a crucifix. African giants hired by the foot, with secret orders to kill Picasso, Italian futurists, who possessed nothing, but a past. Endlessly through the Louis Quinze bush, Erica led that vermilion safari in artistic circles until dizzy with the realization that she was bored, bored open to a new sound, one complete as yet unexplored world, jazz, Africa's other face, stranded—in America, yet to be saved. No Erica anywhere could ignore such a situation; who else can bring the silence so completely? Many. But one must lead.

[AS USUAL]

As usual
   the usual axe
      falls on the usual neck
     in the usual place
      at the usual time
as usual.

TELEGRAM TO ALEX/BAGEL SHOP, NORTH BEACH SF

DEAR ALEX, TOMORROW I AM GOING TO EAT ALL OF THE SUEZ AND PANAMA CANALS, SO PLEASE DO NOT USE YOUR LIGHT & GAS AND REFRAIN FROM EYEBALLING FOR TWO SECONDS, WE HAVE A NEW DEAL FOR CHUCK BAUDELAIRE, THE NEW FRENCH JUNKIE KID TO PAINT SOME TENDER BATHING SUITS ON MA & PA KETTLE AND BEARNOG BAROOCK AND CARNAL SPELLMAN CAN'T COME, SO THERE.

CLAP HANDS, HERE COMES THE LINDBERGH BABY

I reject those frozen
injections
of last night's junk
tragedy,
memory,
blotted survivor
no longer remembers
chromed elbows,
rosy highways,
pinned submission,
eyeless skull faces,
socketless eyes
screwed in,
eyes that have no history,
eyes that darken brows,
eyes that have no lids,
eyes that never blink
broken into &
entered eyes.

Sometimes a sacred dream
is wrapped in a scarf,
circling an anonymous
neck,
hung on a hook.
Sometimes are smoked times,
ambitiously obscured times,
frail times of the long pipe,
Mandarin by implication.

Maybe the young poets
wanted to be popes
or kings
of Mexico.

UNANIMITY HAS BEEN ACHIEVED,
NOT A DOT LESS FOR ITS ACCIDENTALNESS

Raga of the drum, the drum the drum the drum the drum,
the heartbeat
Raga of hold, raga of fold, raga of root, raga of crest, raga
before coming,
Raga of lip, raga of brass, raga of ultimate come with yester-
day, raga of a parched tongue-walked lip, raga of yellow,
raga of mellow, raga of new, raga of old, raga of blue,
raga of gold, raga of air spinning into itself,
I ring against slate and shell and wood and stone and leaf
and bone
And towered holes and floors and eyes—against lone is lorn &
rock & dust & flattened ball & solitudes of air & breath &
hair & skin fed halves & wholes & bulls & calves & mad
& soul & new & old & silence & saves & fall wall & water
falling & fling my eye to sky & tingle & tangle.
I sing a mad raga, I sing a mad raga, a glad raga for the ringing
bell I sing.
A man fishing with old clothes line, shouting bass drum
Sometimes in extravagant moments of shock of unrehearsed
curiosity, I crawl outside myself, sneaking out through the
eyes, one blasé, one surprised, until I begin to feel my own
strangeness; shyly I give up the ghost and go back in until
next time.

I can remember four times when I was not crying & once when
I was not laughing.
I am kneaded by a million black fingers & nothing about me
improves.
Gothic brain surgeons, weeping over the remains of destroyed
love machines.
Diggers, corkscrewing cleanly in, exhilerausted, into the mind
mine, impaled on edgeless shafts of subtle reminiscence,
green-walking across the belts and ties.
Slanted dark-walked time, wet with ages of dryness,

Raga of insignificance & blessed hopelessness.
Raga of sadness, of madness, of green screamed dreams, mile-
deep eyes.

The greatest men have gone unknown: Buddha was the twenty-
fourth.
A beggar is the body of a God-ness, come to shoot movies
with his eye,
Movies of people who do not beg, ragged, broke eagles,
hummed into the wheels turning, some in, others out,
rarely ever in or out, or vice versa, half open.
A string begins where a man ends a string, a man begins where
a string ends. A man bereft of string falls all walls, be-
comes a screamed baby, raved.

FRAGMENT FROM PUBLIC SECRET

REBELS, WHAT ARE REBELS, HERE IN THIS LAND OF REBELLION, THIS LAND THAT BEGAN WITH REBELLION—ARE THEY THOSE WHOSE ACTIVITIES CAN OBJECTIVELY BE ABSORBED OR ASSIMILATED INTO THE PATTERING TIME, REMEMBER, IT IS NOT IMPORTANT, FOR IN THE END, THE REBEL IS TIMELESS, AND IT IS ONLY IN THE PASSAGE OF TIME THAT WE CAN DISCERN THE REBEL FROM THE DISSENTER.

AMERICA, WHO ARE YOUR REBELS, WHAT SHORES HAVE THEY BEEN CAST UPON? IS IT BECAUSE YOU HAVE DISCOVERED A USE FOR EVERYTHING THAT THEY HAVE FOUND THEIR ONLY RECOURSE IS TO SEEK AMONG NOTHING, HOPING TO FIND COMPONENTS WHICH, IN THE FINALITIES OF CONSTRUCTION, MIGHT ASSUME THE POSTURES OF PRINCIPLES, AND DISCOVERING THE HORROR OF FRUSTRATION, TURN TO DEATH AS THE FOUNT OF THE CREATIVE ACT? FROM THERE TO WHERE? WHERE DO SEEKERS GO—SEEKERS WHO HAVE NO GERMAN PHILOSOPHER TO LEAD THEM THROUGH THE HALLS OF DOOM, WHOSE WHITELIKE WALLS ARE INVISIBLE TO THE NAKED EYE? SEEKERS OF THE TRUTH HAVE ALWAYS WAKED EYES, AND ALWAYS WILL, AND IN TIME SHALL BE NAKED IN THEIR OWN LIGHT.

HERE IS A REBEL, ONE LARGE, MONSTROUS REBEL, WHO FIRST TEARS DOWN HIMSELF, AND SNEAKS LIKE FIREWORKS INTO THE PATHS OF OTHERS, HOPING TO EXPLODE, OFTEN SHOWERED, EXISTENT TO THE END.

EVERY TIME I OPEN MY BIG MOUTH
I PUT MY SOUL IN IT.
IT TAKES SO MUCH TO BE NOTHING,
TO SHROUD THE MIND'S EYE
FROM THE GAUDY THEATER
OF THE HEAD.
FALLNESS NOON OF THE MIND
CLUTTERED WITH DISCARDED FANTASIES
NERVE PANELED CORRIDORS OF IMAGINATION
OPENING ON HIDDEN UNIVERSE
GLIMPSED IN THE ECHO
OF A SCREAM.

SCENE IN A THIRD EYE

on the gray shadow of the darkened city
in lost photographs of other sad visions,
ferrying images of transient ecstasies,
pains, private sadnesses, hid
in smoky towers, secret pockets in clandestine
nations.

what? pushed into hungry mouths of crowded buildings
retains its form, reason is too unreliable,
memory screwed into hoped-for visions, desire,
twisted beyond recognition, detected in echoed
sound.
shouting crossviews from worn cliffs, dug down
in the wake of violent earthworms, blinded in
refracted corkscrew glares, from coppery phantom
silhouettes of fake existence, pinned into air, stuck in
time.

NOVELS FROM A FRAGMENT IN PROGRESS

RETURN TRIP SEATED ERECT ON THE SINGING TRAIN IN DELIBERATE ATTEMPT NOT TO FALL ASLEEP, USE OF IMAGINATION TO AVOID SWAYING PEOPLE, UNREAL VISIONS OF MURALS ON RED RESTROOM FLOORS, SLEEP URGE GETTING STRONGER, SCREWING UP THE EYES TO A PERFECT BREAST, ROUGH STOP, STRONG WISH FOR EROTICISM DEPARTING NATIONS CARRYING BIG PAPER BAGS, WONDERING ABOUT THE DENTS IN BOXER'S FACES, REJECTION OF THE SEXUAL ASPECT OF SWEAT, PICTURE OF THE MOTORMAN AS THE MYSTIC FERRYMAN, HIS FACE WOULD EVER BE DESCRIBED IN NOVELS, AWARENESS OF MUSIC OUT BY THE WHEELS, SERIOUS ATTEMPT TO WRITE SONGS, SURPRISED AT MY OWN NAIVETE, AMUSED BY SOUNDS LIKE ONE I CAN'T WRITE, APPROACHING STATION, EYES OF SLIDING DOOR, WAITING FOR IT TO OPEN, MORE PEOPLE, ANOTHER STOP. IT ALWAYS HAPPENS, BRING THIS OFF WITHOUT ANNOYING. ALWAYS WATCH THEM GET OFF BEFORE THE BIG EVENT, I ALMOST GIVE UP AT TIMES LIKE THESE. HOW TO SAVE IT. REPETITIOUS FRUSTRATION, NOW, MYSTIC HOURS WITHOUT LOSING A GRIP ON MY SANITY & FREQUENTLY, WOMEN REALIZE MY CONCENTRATION TO MASTER THIS TRICK, WILLING TO RIDE PAST THEIR DESTINATION.

SECONDLESS

Secondless, minute scarred, hourless, owless, sourness,
  flowerless, for a statement, FOR GOD
the Pygmies are ECSTATIC.
                    FICKLE TIME GONE FROM TIME INTO TIMELESSNESS,
Sometimes are tickless times,
      BILLIE HOLIDAY, UNFUNNY LAUGHTER TIME & HOT WORLDS
      FRECKLED TROPHY TIME
slanted & faded cloudy times,
white stain powdery rock times,
MOUTHMARKED ROCKLESS TIMES
Morning times, salamandered time,
MINUTE AGES OF TIMELESS TIME & CLOCKLESS CLOCKS, &
      COCKLESS COCK.
  Times of many colored afternoons,
WHEN MORNING BECAME A STRANGE HOSPITAL, & DE-TIMED
      THE NEEDLESS DREAM,
time's brilliant alcoves, unbelled,
where brown shadows, snap like slivers
of widowed icycles . . . iced cycles . . .
pale times of riding the crippled horse,
to untimed farthest dry lips of the mind,
hazy latitudes of desperate hours, flattened
into stretching landscapes tickless cinemas,
technicolored on silently curved screens
      of the mind.
BROKEN BY QUIET BLACK LAKES & NERVY GEYSERS &
      NOTHING CONTINUED.
A GREAT PAINTING IS HUNG UP ON THE SKY.
THE ARTIST HIDES IN A JUNGLE OF WRECKED CLOCKS.

[DARKWALKING ENDLESSLY]

DARKWALKING ENDLESSLY, THESE ANGUISHED FLOORS OF EARTH
THROUGH RAINFULL SEASONS OF THE MIND, PAST THE FOAMING
WAVE OF BROKEN INTO AND ENTERED EYES, RIDING BLACK HORSES
TO THE THIN LIPS OF THE MIND. IN A YEAR OF BREAKING
APRILS, I COME TO THAT PLACE THERE. MY SOUL IS MOONBURNED.
MY BODY A SINEWED HURT FOR ALL THE NOTHING THAT I AM,
THE NOTHING THAT IS ALL MY MINGLES OF AFRICAN HAIR.
SPEAK FOR ME. I WEAVE THE WINDS AND KISS THE RAINS,
ALL FOR LOVE.

I DREAMED I DREAMED AN AFRICAN DREAM. MY HEAD WAS A
BONY GUITAR, STRUNG WITH TONGUES, AND PLUCKED BY GOLD
FEATHERED WINGLESS MOONDRIPPED RITUALS UNDER A MIDNIGHT
SUN, DRUMMING HUMAN BEATS FROM THE HEART OF AN EBONY
GODDESS, HUMMING THE MELODIES OF BEING FROM STONE TO BONE
AND FROM SAND ETERNAL. BLUE RAIN FALLING IN SOFT EYEDROPS
FROM NUDE BODIES OF DANCING PLANETS, BEATS OF SCIENCE
PLAYED ON VIBRATED TEETH OF OPEN-MOUTHED AFRICAN
    HARPSICHORDS.
VENUS, THE STAR JAZZER IN TRANSIT, ON FLUTED BARS OF BLACK
LIGHT, DANCING IN THEATERS OF BIRDS STREAMING BEAUTY'S NAME
BEYOND THE BELTS. MAHOGANY GOLDFISH BLOSSOM IN THICKLY
    LOADED
SKIES DOWN FROM THE INTIMATE DISTANCE BY A RIVER WHERE
    PEACE
IS GREEN IN THE FOUNTAIN. ROSES DISAPPEAR INTO EACH OTHER.
THE SUN AND THE MOON CREATE THE BALLAD AT ITS SOURCE, AND
ALL THOSE FIRES OF LOVE I BURN IN MEMORY OF.

HIGHER THAN THE TALLEST PEAKS
DEEPER THAN THE STEEPEST CLOUDS
FARTHER THAN THE FARTHEST SEAS
STANDS THE SERENE KINGDOM OF THE TRULY FAIR
WITH HER IMMORTAL CHILDREN OF
                THE MIND.

THE GREAT ROSE OF TIME TURNS SLOWLY.
THE DREAM FLOWN ON WINGS OF SILVER BELLS, BEYOND HARPOONS
AND SCREECH OWL,
GONE FAR ON BEYOND BEYOND.
THE DREAM IS ON THE HEIGHTS AND RISING.

[I WANT TO ASK A TERRIFYING QUESTION]

I want to ask a terrifying question,
"What time is it going to be?"
That Sunday never came,
He lied, speaking in tongues,
Hot walking New York, in smoky Januaries,

My back is moonburned,
And my arm hurts,
The blues come riding,
Introspective echoes of a journey,
Truth is a burning guitar,
You get off at Fifty-ninth Street forever.

[THE TRAVELING CIRCUS]

The traveling circus crossed the unicorn
with one silver dollar & pederasty eyes.

If i can't be an ugly rumor i won't be the good time had by all.

A certain terror is more rare to me than desirable
than publishing two volumes of my suicide notes,
there are too many lanky baseball players,
newspapering my bathroom floor, and too much
progress in the burial industry, let's go back,
to old-fashioned funerals, & sit around &
be sad, & forgive one another, & go outside
to bury the bottle, & borrow stiff handkerchiefs,
& help load the guy in the wagon & flirt with the widow,
& pretend not to see all those people sinking
into subways, going to basketball games,
going to those basketball games.

A certain desirable terror is more desirable to me than rare
than the thought that i could die right in the middle of
sexual intercourse, & with my new all-purpose transistor
blanket go right on pumping away, with no emotional letdown
if you stop, you're dead, the jakov syndrome, tell the kids,
don't mess around with the light switch, tell them they'll
        be shocked
if they unplug daddy.

A terror is more certain that's rare, & more desirable.

THERE ARE TOO MANY UNFUNNY THINGS HAPPENING TO THE
        COMEDIANS.
Why don't the monasteries serve hot & cold hero sandwiches &
all kinds of split pea soups, & bring the guys to the village
once a week to get laid, & make them stop printing all those fat

books with god's picture on the cover,
& all that subway mystery stuff.

A certain desire is more rare than terror,
than that happy shop, home of free association,
where i breakfasted with the suicidal rabbi,
& the world's champion padlock salesman, who
wore impeccable seersuckers, & whose only
oversight is cannibalism, & who is someday going
to eat himself and get busted if he stays in the
flesh game.

All bicycle seats beatified & take on appearance of north poles,
        other things
certain are real to me, but what is so rare, as air is a poem.

It's all right real, it's just god playing dirty jokes again,
that was the old universal gin mill story, with chopin &
amelia earhart floating down the suez canal with dueling pistols
in their hair, as the great symphony of fish play beethoven's
        teeth.

TRANSACTION

TO BREAK THE SPELL OF SUNDAY
I OFFERED THE GANGSTER A SILK EAR
AND FIRST COPIES OF FAMOUS HOROSCOPES.
HE DEMANDED AN UNWRITTEN CONTRACT
WITNESSED BY A GYPSY QUEEN.

BLUES FOR HAL WATERS

My head, my secret cranial guitar, strung with myths plucked
    from
Yesterday's straits, it's buried in robes of echoes, my eyes,
    breezeless bags, lacquered to present a glint . . .
My marble lips, entrance to that cave, where visions renounce
    renunciation,
Eternity has wet sidewalks, angels are busted for drunk flying.
I only want privacy to create an illusion of me blotted out.
His high hopes were placed in his coffin. Long paddles of
    esteem for his symbol canoe.
If I move to the stars, forward my mail c/o God, Heaven,
    Lower East Side.
Too late for skindiving and other modern philosophies, put my
    ego in storage.
The moon is too near my family, and the craters are cold in
    winter,
Let's move to the sun, hot water, radiant heating, special
    colors,
Knife-handle convenience, adjacent to God, community
    melting free.
Eskimos have frozen secrets in their noses and have chopped
    down the North Pole.
The Last Buffalo will be torpedoed by an atomic submarine,
    firing hydrogen tiepins.
God is my favorite dictator, even though he refuses to hold
    free elections.
I worry about the padlock I painted on.
My hair is overrun with crabgrass, parts of my anatomy are still
    unexplored.
No more harp sessions for me; I am going to hell and hear
    some good jazz.
Do you hear the good news, Terry and the Pirates are not
    really real.
If you value the comfort of your fellow worshippers, don't die
    in church.

28

Why ruin our eyes with TV, let's design freeways after dinner
   tonight.

He might have lost some friends, but Jesus could have made
   a fortune on that water to wine formula.
History is the only diary God keeps, and somebody threw it
   on the bonfire.
The day of the Big Game at Hiroshima. The moon is a double
   agent.
This year the animals are holding their first
   "Be kind to people" week.
The Siamese cats will not participate and will hold their own
   convention in Egypt. The civilized world fears they may
   attempt to put Pharoah back in place on the throne.
For God's sake, Hal, jam the radio. Trip them with your guitar.

A TIGER IN EACH KNEE

White tiger I hear your
Hum on the drone
Flowing on beds of
Fresh snow on springs
Flowing back to the nether
        source,
The truth is an empty
        bowl of rice
Those cathode men who cage
    you shall melt
In the summer sun,
For they are ugly bars
Who echo the sting of
Unholy rivers in their dried cracked
Bed.

WALK SOUNDS

Soft noise, where crystalline sap dwells.
Tree bark houses, tree bark shoes.
Long green journeys, into sounds of death.
Cries of who blows, who blows, who blows,
Rings of raindrops, on damp streets.
Quietly disappearing, in fearmottled night,
Sweeping over asphalt mesas, to long gutters,
Where gray birds lie, gone time is buried,
Safe from hideous laughter, babblings,
Of sidewalk fools, tongues straining,
Flicking, on steps of air, nervously.
Glowing blue, black, blue, black,
In the shapes of night.

WAR MEMOIR:
JAZZ, DON'T LISTEN TO IT AT YOUR OWN RISK

In the beginning, in the wet
Warm dark place,
Straining to break out, clawing at strange cables
Hearing her screams, laughing
"Later we forgot ourselves, we didn't know"
Some secret jazz
Shouted, wait, don't go.
Impatient, we came running, innocent
Laughing blobs of blood and faith.
To this mother, father world
Where laughter seems out of place
So we learned to cry, pleased
They pronounced human.
The secret jazz blew a sigh
Some familiar sound shouted wait
Some are evil, some will hate.
"Just Jazz, blowing it's top again"
So we rushed and laughed.
As we pushed and grabbed
While Jazz blew in the night
Suddenly we were too busy to hear a sound
We were busy shoving mud in men's mouths,
Who were busy dying on living ground
Busy earning medals, for killing children on deserted
     streetcorners
Occupying their fathers, raping their mothers, busy humans
     were
Busy burning Japanese in atomicolorcinescope
With stereophonic screams,
What one-hundred-percent red-blooded savage would waste
     precious time
Listening to Jazz, with so many important things going on
But even the fittest murderers must rest

So we sat down on our blood-soaked garments,
And listened to Jazz
                    lost, steeped in all our dreams
We were shocked at the sound of life, long gone from our own
We were indignant at the whistling, thinking, singing, beating,
    swinging
Living sound, which mocked us, but let us feel sweet life again
We wept for it, hugged, kissed it, loved it, joined it, we
        drank it,
Smoked it, ate with it, slept with it
We made our girls wear it for lovemaking
Instead of silly lace gowns,
Now in those terrible moments, when the dark memories come
The secret moments to which we admit no one
When guiltily we crawl back in time, reaching away from
        ourselves
We hear a familiar sound,
Jazz, scratching, digging, bluing, swinging jazz,
And we listen
And we feel
And live.

ARRIVAL

Bitter rose blood from dead grapes,
Miniature rivers, flowing on cracked lips.
Old men fighting death in secret corners,
Time rushing wildly through terrified streets.

Odors of laughter reach the nostrils,
Pure poetry from the mouths of children,
Waves of dark flames batter the dawn.
The crawling day arrives, on skinned
Knees.

LIKE FATHER, LIKE SUN

Come, Love,
Love, Come,
Sing a river, Federico . . . García . . . Lorca . . .
In Sarah's tents a Gypsy moon . . . Godless Spain's burning
noon . . .
I wrote my first poem in brown gravy, my best friend was
a green candle,
Orleans . . . New Orleans . . . the bend in the river cleaves
to the sky . . .
Louisiana, named for a broken sun king, bequeathed to a star
jazzer,
Miro . . . the flowers are still up there on that wall, stem,
petal, all,
Their roots playing the silences, between Babatunde's
drumbeats,
Feeding pongee petals to green breezes, flying in darting
wonder.
Crane, the flowers have crossed your bridge, beyond, beyond;
gone far on
When the wind is blowing through my hair, I cry breath, its
coolness loves.
The great rose of time turns on her redding breast,
Pocahontas's here,
The land is Apache, Kiowa, and Sioux ranges.
Colorado brings a horse.
The white tiger's horn growls—the drone, the man he killed
who caged him . . .
They are ugly bars, who echo the sting of unholy rivers, zoos
of death,
The poet in Easter-faced boots, walks from my chest, mystic
bloodfruit.
Be the hum in the cluster.
Muddy Mississippi flowing to the thickly hooded skin, cross
the bar,

Andean the Delta counts the teeth in the Buddha's smile,
    vanishing directions,
Whispers, the great rain forest grows mahogany goldfish,
    Africa's stolen babes,
Coming from ages of impalement, ages wet with dryness,
    awesome of soul.
Their right eye is a sun, their left eye is a moon.
Their blue eyes come walking, introspective echoes of
    a journey, soaring,
Of the first generation, the first humans, their cradle
    the shape of
The human heart, its sound comes in color of the moon, the sun
Returns their golden crown, wrapped in the aura of familiarity,
    bathed
In want and care, dank bare, safe in compassion's attic.
Beyond harpoons and screech owls and ringless bells.
Europe, the hornless bull, eunuch rapist of infants, man
    and God,
Whines stench of king time as Joan's light flickers, and
    goes out,
Gone to herald her father's shore,
Who in her descent from the peak, found the summits in
    mankind's suffering breast.
The liars who stole the soul do not notice, their hearts no
    longer beat, they cannot die, they are in hell now,
Their Power, fungus and rainless soon,
Michelangelo screaming in lonely triumph,
The sound that probes to the
Otherside.
The poem comes
Across centuries of holy lies, and weeping heaven's eyes,
Africa's black handkerchief, washed clean by her children's
    honor,
As cruelly designed anniversaries spin in my mind,
Airy voice of all those fires of love I burn in memory of.

America is a promised land, a garden torn from naked stone,
A place where the losers in earth's conflicts can enjoy
    their triumph.
All losers, brown, red, black, and white; the colors from the
    Master Palette.

MORNING JOY

Piano buttons, stitched on morning lights.
Jazz wakes with the day,
As I awaken with jazz, love lit the night.
Eyes appear and disappear,
To lead me once more, to a green moon.
Streets paved with opal sadness,
Lead me counterclockwise, to pockets of joy,
And jazz.

BONSAI POEMS

I

I remember those days before I knew of my soul's existence.
I used to be able to step on bugs and steal flowers.

II

All those well-meaning people who gave me obscure books
When what I really needed was a good meal.

III

Lately, since formulating mystic parables of my own,
People ask me what do I know all about China—
And do I think Surrealism will spread to Iowa—
Or would winning the Pulitzer Prize have saved Chessman,
When I answer that I am writing the Great American Suicide
     Note,
They sniff my clothes and leave.

IV

Men who love women
Should never go swimming.

V

Every time I see an old man carrying a shabby cardboard
     suitcase,
I think he is an eternity agent on some secret mission.

VI

I never understand other people's hopes or desires
Until they coincide with my own; then we clash.

VII

Yes, there was a time when I was unsure of myself,
But that was before I was Me. I barely knew him.

VIII

The culture of the cave man disappeared, due to his inability
To produce a magazine that could be delivered by a kid on
a bicycle.

DEMOLITION

They have dismantled
The Third Avenue El;
It's still the same though,
They haven't removed
Those torn-down men.

QUERY

New? Leftovers, overlooked by hurrying death.
Rejects with unadjustable souls,
Love-specked clots, of modern blood.

Marks, all over inside,
Traces of explosions,
First God's, then man's.

Color? Blue, jazz blue.
Blue like love,
Blue like poems,
Blue like blues.

Old? Whole university loads,
Tons of cellophane giants.
Book-end minds, bent backs,
Carrying heavy styles,
Lead forms, tradition colored.
Shouting barbarian, blasphemy,
But quite polite.

New:
     Laughter on exotic beds.

SPLICED REFLECTIONS

Diverse remarks on what is truly dead
(Success and crime, two equal values).

Historical departure (Cain's refusal to slay Abel)
Persistence of women who still love.

Voice of unseen commentary heard through plugged ears,
Obscure history of grass fires (Niagara of Soul).

Grunt passage (navigating in blocked wombs).

Sudden conference with imaginary Indian chiefs
(Ritual smoking, floors of white buffalo skins).

Innocent criminals buried under avalanches of cactus needles
(Great philosophical question: Was Geronimo turned on?)

Inca arrival, sun-faced jaguars, hammered-silver evidence,
Testimonial rockets launched (commemoration of
Baudelaire's whims).

Cold penetration is unison (arid tests of burning mollusk)
Ritual murder and levitation, semiweekly mating dances.

Light the wind, drag the rain in.

THE CELEBRATED WHITE-CAP SPELLING BEE

THE CELEBRATED WHITE-CAP SPELLING BEE WAS WON BY A
SPELLING BEE.

A STAR ASKED A POINTED QUESTION: CAN A CIRCLE WRAP AROUND
ITSELF?

A STILLED PYGMY ANSWERS, FROM THE BACK OF MY MIND, ARE WE
DEEP DWARFS

AND HAVE OUR SAY IN THE AFFAIRS OF FLOWERS. A MISSPELLLED BEE
MAKES A SIGN.

BLUE IS ONE OF THE MANY FACES OF BLUE. HOW QUICK A RED WHALE
SINGS THE BLUES.

WHEN AN OUTBOARD SOLAR BOAT SINKS, I WILL WALK THE SUN'S
PERIMETER, CURVING UP.

ONCE I PUT MY INITIALS ON A MAGNIFICENT CROCODILE.

WE WALKED A RIVER'S FLOOR. A BIRD I HEARD SING IN A TREE IN THE
GULF OF MEXICO . . .

BIRD SONG OF LOVELY SALT, A LOVE SONG.

I CHANGE MY MIND, AND THE NEW ONE IS OLDER . . . A DRUM BEATS
BEHIND MY RIBS.

SOMEONE DREW A PORTRAIT ON A WAVE . . . IT WOVE AS WE
PASSED, DOING KNOTS, RUST HANDS.

SWELLS STOP WHEN THE SEA IS ALARMED. HELL COOLS ITS FIRES OF
ANTICIPATION.

WHEN OCEANS MEET, OCEANS BELOW, REUNIONS OF SHIPS, SAILORS,
GULLS, BLACK-HAIRED GIRLS.

THE SEA BATHES IN RAIN WATER, MORNING, MOON & LIGHT, THE
CLEAN SEA.

GREAT FARMS ON THE OCEAN FLOOR, GREEN CROPS OF SUNKEN HULLS
GROWING SHELLS.

SEAS THAT GROW FROM A HOLE BORN IN A TURTLE'S BACK, A SEA IN
A TORTOISE SACK.

FISH GO NAKED ALL THEIR LIVES. WHEN CAUGHT, THEY DIE OF
EMBARRASSMENT.

MANY, MANY YEARS AGO, THERE WERE MANY, MANY YEARS TO GO
& MANY, MANY MILES TO COME.

THE LAND IS A GREAT, SAD FACE. THE SEA IS A HUGE TEAR,
COMPASSION'S TWINS.

IF THERE IS A GOD BENEATH THE SEA, HE IS DRUNK AND TELLING
FANTASTIC LIES.
WHEN THE MOON IS DRINKING, THE SEA STAGGERS LIKE A DRUNKEN
SAILOR.
POETS WHO DROWN AT SEA, THEMSELVES, BECOME BEAUTIFUL WET
SONGS, CRANE.
A LOOKOUT MAKES A LANDFALL, A FALLING LAND MAKES A LOOKOUT.
AT THE ENDS OF THE WATER, THE HOLY MARRIAGE OF THE HORIZONS.
THE SEA, DILUTED CONTINENTS LOVING FALLEN SKIES, TIME BEFORE
TIME, TIME PAST, TIME COMING INTO TIME. TIME NOW, TIME
TO COME, TIMELESS, FLOWING INTO TIME.
EVERYTHING IS THE SEA. THE SEA IS EVERYTHING, ALWAYS . . .
ETERNALLY, I SWEAR.

THE SECRET LIFE OF ROBERT FROST

FROCK-COATED SHERPA GUIDES DISTRIBUTING (MONOGRAMMED
    GOLDFISH)
TO NEGLECTED MIDWIVES AT SECRET TRYST ON DESERTED ROLLER
    (COASTERS)

DEMENTED ELEVATOR OPERATORS IN SPACE SUITS SINGING HYMNS
TO GOTHIC BRAIN SURGEONS WEEPING OVER REMAINS OF DESTROYED
LOVE MACH(I)NES, O ULTIMA THULE (NO) MORE OAT(ME)AL.

DEVOTED TUNE PICKERS WHINING OF VANISHED TRIUMPHS
DRESSED IN SURREALIST TUNICS OF GAUZE AND IVORY
RUBBER PHANTOMS TAPPING UNFANTASTIC CRIMINAL FEET
TO WARPED RHYTHMS SHOT FROM OPEN-SKULLED HARPSICHORDS
GALA LAUNDRY CONCERTS FEATURING SONATAS FOR DIRTY OBOES
    BETWEEN MUSHROOM RONDOS' SOGGY BALLETS
SERVED WITH PERFUMED MARSHMALLOWS FROM KEY EYES OF
    LONELY JAZZERS.

TORN ASPHALT MATTRESS OF UNIVERSAL RODENTS (PSYCHIC
    IMPOTENCE)
COLLEGE FACES OF GRANITE ANTIQUITIES STALKED BY LAZY TIGERS
    (STRIPES)
SMELLY BROADCASTS OF COMIC TRAGEDIES BURST FROM FLOWER
    DUST (SKULLS)
COOL DAMP TONGUES SLIPPED FROM LIPS OF SKINNY (LOUDSPEAKERS)
CROUCHED BEHIND CLASSIC FACES OF MYSTIC (TRAFFIC) LIGHTS
    BLAZING
HARD COLD WAVES OF TINSEL FROM BEADS OF KIDNAPPED LAMAS
BURNING OLD PRAYER WHEELS IN ABANDONED (PHONE BOOTHS)
ACHING TEMPOS DRIPPING FROM MOANING (AFRICAN (FINGERS OF ART
                       ART)   BLAKEY)
ABSTRACT BOMBS DROPPING FROM SWOLLEN BELLIES (OF BLASTED
    EGGSHELLS)
FLOATING DOWN BLACK WATER CANALS IN MARBLE BOATS, HIGH ON
                    (SAINTLY   (DESTRUCTION
                    RED DIRT)   MARIJUANA)

[POEMS POETICALLY]

Poems poetically
pole the Poet into a
balancing axis
for endlessly revolving surfaces,
tender leaves are forest gifts
to represent the earth
growing out of decay,
the minds' youngest buds
live on the revolving transformation
of live enduring mountains of thought, and
clear their pores in the melting sea.
And open fields spawn
their harvest in the passing
rain of the plain, as
the spring divines its
collections to the ocean,
and the great waters
continual upheavings speed toward subtle gatherings.
Shepherds with light fingers,
staff guided by the winds,
spinning their
auras into the
sun.

47

ALL HALLOWS, JACK O'LANTERN WEATHER, NORTH OF TIME

A PLACE CALLED LONELINESS, A SOFT TOWN IN THE OCTOBER COUNTRY AN UNIMAGINARY LANDSCAPE THAT EXISTS IN A REAL UNREAL WORLD, ARTERIAL LAVA STREETS CLICKING A SOUND OF LOUDLY WALKED BRUISES THICK STRING UNBEINGS, POURING THEM-SELVES INTO EACH OTHER, FILLING THEMSELVES WITH EACH OTHERS' EMPTINESS, SHOUTING SILENCES ACROSS THE SCREAMING ROOMS, VISUALLY BROKEN UNRECORDS STITCHING ILLUSIONARY HUMS, AS THE GREAT MARBLE FEATHERED STONE BIRDS CRACK THE SOLID AIR, FLYING FROM THE DRUM OF ROCK, ETERNAL STONE POEM OF THE SUN . . . I KNOW OF A PLACE IN BETWEEN BETWEEN, BEHIND BEHIND, IN FRONT OF FRONT, BELOW BELOW, ABOVE ABOVE, INSIDE INSIDE, OUTSIDE OUTSIDE, CLOSE TO CLOSE, FAR FROM FAR, MUCH FARTHER THAN FAR, MUCH CLOSER THAN CLOSE, ANOTHER SIDE OF AN OTHER SIDE . . . IT LIES OUT ON THE FAR SIDE OF MUSIC . . . THAT DARKLING PLANE OF LIGHT ON THE OTHER SIDE OF TIME, AND IT GOES ON GOING ON BEYOND BEYOND . . . IT BEGINS AT THE BITTER ENDS.
I KNOW STARNESS . . . I KNOW LOSTNESS . . . MOVE OUT MOON-LIGHT.

RONDEAU OF THE ONE SEA

DEEP ROLLING GALILEE, ETERNAL SEVEN OCEAN NAMED SEA END-
LESSLY FLOWING HOLY SEA, SEA NEVER STILLED, ALL FLOWING SEA,
SEA DESTROYER OF BAAL AND MAMMON, DRIED AND FOREVER DRIED
SEA, SEA, ERASER OF SEA DARKS, REMOVER OF SEA VALVES, EVAPO-
RATOR OF THE EVIL ONES PARENT OCEAN SEA, SEA BREAKER OF RA'S
SEA, BROKEN AND DEHYDRATED FOREVER BY DEEP ROLLING GALILEE,
SWEET GREEN WET BLUE SALTLESS SEA: BELOVED GALILEE, THE
GREEN WALKING, BLUE WALKING JESUS CHRIST, SEA.

BLOOD FELL ON THE MOUNTAINS

BLUENESS, THE COLOR OF LOVE, BLUE SLANTED TO A CRACKLING AND
BLUE COLOR, THE COLOR OF COLORS AS SWEET BLUE NOCTURNES OF
THE VOID. SOLITUDES FILLED WITH LONELINESS, BLACK RAIN TWISTED
HAIL, WOUNDED SNOW.
THE MOUNTAIN CRIED DRY, TEAR OF STONE AMONG THE TALL TREES,
THE SLEEPWALKER WALKED THE BRIDGE OF EYES, AMIDST COLORS OF
THE DAY.

        IN THE LEFT HAND IS THE DREAMER
        THE BALLAD AT THE SOURCE
        THE SINGER AND THE SONG,
        POEM FOR EILEEN ON MY
        RETURN HOME,

        I   AM   A   LOVER
                BOB
        ME   TO   YOU.

SMALL MEMORIAM FOR MYSELF

Beyond the reach of scorn, lust is freed of its vulgar face.
No more blanch of terror at reality's threat of sadness.
No blend of grief can cause the death of laughter now.

In remembrance of certain lights I have seen go out,
I have visualized pathetic rituals and noisy requiems,
Composed of metaphysical designs of want and care.

NEW POEMS
1973–1978

[ALL THOSE SHIPS THAT NEVER SAILED]

All those ships that never sailed
The ones with their seacocks open
That were scuttled in their stalls . . .
Today I bring them back
Huge and intransitory
And let them sail
Forever.

All those flowers that you never grew—
    that you wanted to grow
The ones that were plowed under
    ground in the mud—
Today I bring them back
And let you grow them
Forever.

All those wars and truces
Dancing down these years—
All in three flag-swept days
Rejected meaning of God—

My body once covered with beauty
Is now a museum of betrayal.
This part remembered because of that one's touch
This part remembered for that one's kiss—
Today I bring it back
And let you live forever.

I breathe a breathless I love you
And move you
Forever.

Remove the snake from Moses' arm . . .

And someday the Jewish queen will dance
Down the street with the dogs
And make every Jew
Her lover.

[MY MYSTERIES CREATED FOR ME]

MY MYSTERIES CREATED FOR ME
BY GOD ARE UNKNOWN TO
ME, YET I LIVE EACH ONE
PERFECTLY, GOD IS MY GREEN-
EYED ONE, WHOSE POWER IS
ENDLESS. I ASK GOD,
OH GOD . . . TO THE COWARD, GIVE A HORSE
THAT HE MAY FLEE GOD FOREVER,
GIVE CAIN NO FORGIVENESS
FOR WHAT WAS DONE, I ASK GOD,
MY GREEN-EYED ONE, BEFORE THIS
EARTH STOPS SPINNING, THINK OF ME.
REMEMBER, I AM HERE TOO, MY GREEN-
EYED ONE WHOSE POWER IS ENDLESS, AFTER
WHAT WAS DONE TO YOU, WHAT FORGIVENESS . . .
O GOD, MY GREEN-EYED ONE
COME UPON THE EARTH
AND STRIKE THE GLOBE
WITH YOUR WRATH, FOR
WHAT HAS DIED IN THE SUN.
O GOD, MY GREEN-EYED ONE,
PUT YOUR SHARP STARS IN
THE SKY. SEND ORION
THE HUNTER STAR TO HUNT
THE KILLERS OF THE DREAM,
TO HUNT THE SLAYERS OF
THE DIVINE INCUNABULA, O
MY GREEN-EYED ONE, BEFORE THIS EARTH STOPS
SPINNING.

OREGON

You are with me Oregon,
Day and night, I feel you, Oregon.
I am Negro. I am Oregon.
Oregon is me, the planet
Oregon, the State Oregon, Oregon.
In the night, you come with bicycle wheels,
Oregon you come
With stars of fire. You come green.
Green eyes, hair, arms,
Head, face, legs, feet, toes
Green, nose green, your
Breast green, your cross
Green, your blood green.
Oregon winds blow around
Oregon. I am green, Oregon.
You are mine, Oregon. I am yours,
Oregon. I live in Oregon.
Oregon lives in me,
Oregon, you come and make
Me into a bird and fly me
To secret places day and night.
The secret places in Oregon,
I am standing on the steps
Of the holy church of Crispus
Attucks St. John the Baptist,
The holy brother of Christ,
I am talking to Lorca. We
Decide the Hart Crane trip, home to Oregon
Heaven flight from Gulf of
Mexico, the bridge is
Crossed, and the florid black found.

UNTITLED

THE SUN IS A NEGRO.
THE MOTHER OF THE SUN IS A NEGRO.
THE DISCIPLES OF THE
SUN ARE NEGRO.
THE SAINTS OF THE
SUN ARE NEGRO.
HEAVEN IS NEGRO.

[THE NIGHT THAT LORCA COMES]

THE NIGHT THAT LORCA COMES
SHALL BE A STRANGE NIGHT IN THE
SOUTH, IT SHALL BE THE TIME WHEN NEGROES LEAVE THE SOUTH
    FOREVER,
GREEN TRAINS SHALL ARRIVE
FROM RED PLANET MARS
CRACKLING BLUENESS SHALL SEND TOOTH-COVERED CARS FOR THEM
TO LEAVE IN, TO GO INTO
THE NORTH FOREVER, AND I SEE MY LITTLE GIRL MOTHER
AGAIN WITH HER CROSS THAT
IS NOT BURNING, HER SKIRTS
OF BLACK, OF ALL COLORS, HER AURA
OF FAMILIARITY. THE SOUTH SHALL WEEP
BITTER TEARS TO NO AVAIL,
THE NEGROES HAVE GONE
INTO CRACKLING BLUENESS.
CRISPUS ATTUCKS SHALL ARRIVE WITH THE BOSTON
COMMONS, TO TAKE ELISSI LANDI
NORTH, CRISPUS ATTUCKS SHALL
BE LAYING ON BOSTON COMMONS,
ELISSI LANDI SHALL FEEL ALIVE
AGAIN. I SHALL CALL HER NAME
AS SHE STEPS ON TO THE BOSTON
COMMONS, AND FLIES NORTH FOREVER,
LINCOLN SHALL BE THERE,
TO SEE THEM LEAVE THE
SOUTH FOREVER, ELISSI LANDI, SHE WILL BE
GREEN.
THE WHITE SOUTH SHALL GATHER AT
PRESERVATION HALL.

THE AMERICAN SUN

THE AMERICAN SUN HAS RISEN,
THE OTHER SUNS HAVE LEFT
THE SKY, THE POEM HAS ENTERED
THE REALM OF BLOOD. BLOOD IS
NOW FLOWING IN ALL SKIES AND
ALL THE STARS CALL FOR MORE
BLOOD, THE OLD EMPIRES HAVE
BEEN BROKEN BY THE AMERICAN
SUN AND SHALL CEASE TO EXIST
AS THE POLITICAL ENTITIES THEY
ONCE WERE, AND CAN NEVER BE
AGAIN, THE AMERICAN SUN
BRINGS DEATH TO ALL ENEMY
EMPIRES, THE AMERICAN SUN BRINGS
DEATH BY FIRE TO ALL WHO DARE
OPPOSE THE AMERICAN SUN, EMPIRES
OF THE PAST ARE BREAKING FROM
THE CONSTANT POWER OF THE AMERICAN
SUN, THE AMERICAN SUN CHALLENGES
ALL OTHER EMPIRES AND DEMANDS
THEY RESPOND TO THE CHALLENGES
OF THE AMERICAN SUN, THOSE THAT DO
NOT RESPOND ARE TO BE BROKEN AND
BURNED, THE AMERICAN SUN
OPENS THE GRAVES OF EMPIRES
THAT FALL TO THE AMERICAN SUN,
ALL FORMER KINGS AND QUEENS
OF EMPIRES CRUSHED BY THE
AMERICAN SUN ARE TAKEN FROM
THEIR GRAVE AND TOMBS TO EXIST
IN THE NIGHT OF THE LIVING
DEAD AND SUFFER THEIR
FALL TO THE AMERICAN SUN,
THE PRIESTS OF THE AMERICAN SUN

ARE STARS IN THE SKIES OF
ALL ENEMY EMPIRES, THEY ADMINISTER
THE LAWS OF THE AMERICAN SUN,
THE AMERICAN SUN DOES NOT GIVE
MERCY TO EMPIRES FALLEN TO
THE AMERICAN SUN,
THE AMERICAN SUN DOES NOT PERMIT
DISOBEDIENCE, ANY ATTEMPT TO
DISOBEY THE AMERICAN SUN
IS PUNISHED BY DEATH AND TOTAL
DESTRUCTION OF THE OFFENDING EMPIRE,
THE AMERICAN SUN IS THE
ONLY SUN, ALL OTHERS ARE
BROKEN AND TORN FROM THE
SKY BY THE AMERICAN SUN,
THE DARK STAR THE ENEMY SUNS
HAVE BECOME HAS BEEN
THROWN DOWN ON THE ENEMY'S OWN LAND
BY THE AMERICAN SUN.
THE LANGUAGE OF THE AMERICAN
SUN IS SPOKEN BY STARMEN
AND STARWOMEN OF AMERICA,
THE AMERICAN SUN IS AMERICA, AND
ALL AMERICANS. NO OTHERS
ARE PERMITTED ON OR IN THE
AMERICAN SUN. THE AMERICAN
SUN IS THE ONLY FIRE. ALL OTHERS
ARE PUT OUT BY THE AMERICAN
SUN. THE MOON IS THE AMERICAN
MIDNIGHT SUN AND MUST BE
OBEYED BY ALL OTHER EMPIRES,
THE AMERICAN SUN DOES NOT FORGIVE
ANY ENEMY, BUT PUNISHES EVERY OFFENDER
WITH DEATH AND DESTRUCTION.
THE AMERICAN SUN IS AMERICAN
HOLINESS, THE AMERICAN SUN IS

THE SUN OF HEAVEN, THE AMERICAN SUN
IS THE AMERICAN CHURCH, THE AMERICAN
SUN IS AMERICAN RELIGION, THE
AMERICAN SUN IS THE LAW, IN ALL
SKIES, THE AMERICAN
SUN IS AT WAR WITH ALL ENEMIES
OF THE AMERICAN SUN, THE AMERICAN
PLANETS, MARS JUPITER, SATURN VENUS,
PLUS THE OTHER PLANETS OF
THE AMERICAN UNIVERSE ARE
AT WAR WITH ALL OTHER UNIVERSES,
THE AMERICAN SUN CREATES ALL AMERICAN LIFE.
THE AMERICAN SUN CREATES ATOMIC
DEATH ON ALL ENEMIES OF THE SUN, THE AMERICAN
SUN CALLED THE ATOMIC BOMB IS
BEING DROPPED ON ALL ENEMY
CITIES BY THE AMERICAN SUN,
CALLED THE SPIRIT OF ST. LOUIS,
THE AMERICAN SUN CALLED
THE HYDROGEN BOMB, IS BEING
DROPPED ON ALL ENEMY EMPIRES
BY THE AMERICAN SUN, CALLED
THE SPIRIT OF ST. LOUIS, THE
ENEMIES OF THE AMERICAN
SUN ARE NOT PERMITTED TO
SURRENDER, THE AMERICAN SUN
IS DESTROYING ALL ENEMY EMPIRES,
WHEN THE AMERICAN SUN
HAS COMPLETED THE DESTRUCTION
OF ALL ENEMY EMPIRES, THE
AMERICAN SUN SHALL CREATE
THE FIRES OF WAR, BURNING
ALL OVER AND UNDER THE SKIES
OF THE CRUCIFIXION, AT THE
AMERICAN SUN CALLED THE
CROSS, THE BUDDHA HAS BEEN

TOPPLED AND HAS BECOME AN
EASTERN IDOL WITH NO WESTERN
SKY, THE BUDDHA IS NOW STANDING
IN FRONT OF THE AMERICAN SUN CALLED
R.C.A. VICTOR, LISTENING TO HIS MASTER'S VOICE.
THE BUDDHA HAS A BLACK SPOT ON ONE EAR NOW.
THE AMERICAN SUN CALLED
ARTHUR FARNSWORTH TELEVISION
HAS TORN DOWN THE TEMPLE'S
WALLS AND DRIVEN THE MONEY-
LENDERS FROM THE WESTERN
SIDE OF THE RHINE RIVER TO
THE EASTERN SIDE OF THE RIVER
THAT DIVIDES THE GERMAN EMPIRE
INTO TWO SEPARATE BUT EQUAL
STATES, THE AMERICAN SUN HAS
MADE THE MONEYLENDERS
ERECT A WALL OF THE TORN-DOWN
TEMPLE OF THE EAST BANK OF THE RIVER
TO SHIFT THE MONEYLENDER'S POWER
TO THE SIDE OF THE RIVER THAT IS NEAR
VIENNA.
THE AMERICAN SUN CALLED
THE CATHOLIC CHURCH HAS
EXCOMMUNICATED SAVONAROLA
VLADIMIR ILYICH LENIN AND HAS
FORBIDDEN THE RUSSIAN EMPIRE
TO HAVE A CHURCH, OR A CHRISTIAN
RELIGION, THE RELIGIOUS COURT
OF HEAVEN HAS PRONOUNCED HIS
BEHEADING OF THE LADY POPE
ST. JOAN, AN UNFORGIVABLE SIN,
HEAVEN FORBIDS RUSSIA TO HAVE
A CATHOLIC CHURCH, HEAVEN UNDRESSES
THE BODY OF LENIN IN THE TOMB AND
DISCOVERS THE LEGS HAVE TURNED BLACK,
RUSSIAN COMMUNISM IS REFUSED THE

64

SACRAMENT BY HEAVEN, PRINCE MIKE ROMANOV
OF HOLLYWOOD IS THE ONLY RUSSIAN HEAVEN ALLOWS
IN HEAVEN'S CATHOLIC CHURCH
THE AMERICAN SUN CALLED
THE AMERICAN FLAG IS THE
ONLY FLAG FLYING AT CRUCIFIXION
CALLED THE EARTH NOW IN THE
SKIES OF HEAVEN.
THE AMERICAN SUN IS NOT
PART OF ANY PEACE MOVEMENT.
THE AMERICAN SUN IS A
SUN OF WAR, THE DAYS OF
PEACE ARE DRAWING
TO AN END. THE ENEMIES OF
THE AMERICAN SUN ON THE
EARTH SHALL SOON BE ATTACKED
BY THE PURE POWERS OF THE
AMERICAN SUN. THE ENEMIES OF
THE AMERICAN SUN IN AMERICA
HAVE ALREADY BEEN SENT TO
HELL AT THE AMERICAN
CRUCIFIXION. HELL IS CALLED
THX 1138, THE ENEMIES OF
THE AMERICAN SUN ARE SHOWN
THEMSELVES ON TELEVISION,
IT IS FILMED INSIDE THE CROSS
BY THE AMERICAN SUN.
UNLIKE BIRTH OF A NATION,
IT IS NOT IN PUBLIC DOMAIN,
AT THE CRUCIFIXION,
THE AMERICAN SUN HAS
ATTACKED RUSSIA WITH
NUCLEAR WEAPONS AND MOSCOW
IS IN FLAMES, THE TOMB OF
LENIN HAS BEEN DESTROYED,
THE BODY OF LENIN IS BEING CARRIED THROUGH
THE CITY . . .

UNTITLED

THE EARTH MOVED, AND CHANGED ITS
ANGLE IN RELATION TO OTHER UNIVERSES,
THE SPHINX OPENS THE DOOR, HORUS ENTERS
HIS BEAK EMERGES FROM THE SUN OF
HIS HEAD, HORUS ARMS OUTSTRETCHED
GIVES THE POEM A SUBSTANCE, SET GOES OFF.
THE TIME OF SET WAS SHORT, HORUS IS
HERE FOREVER, HORUS ADMIRES THE
GOLD KING, PHAROAH TUTANKHAMEN,
AMON RA STANDS WITH OSIRIS AT KARNAK,
HORUS DIRECTS BOY HORUS TO
THE FLIGHT, PYLON GENTLE FLIGHT,
PRUFROCK ENTERS THE
DOOR TO THE ORIENT
AND EMERGES SWIMMING.

FROM A PAINTING BY EL GRECO

I AM THE ETERNITY THAT WAS HELD
BY THE OSTRICH EGG.
THE MAGNIFICENT DECEMBER IS NOW
NO LONGER HIDDEN.
THE SUN, I AM ALONE, IS PRESENT FOREVER.

THE POET

FROM A PIT OF BONES
THE HANDS OF CREATION
FORM THE MIND, AND SHAPE
THE BODY IN LESS THAN A SECOND.
    A FISH WITH FROG'S
    EYES,
    CREATION IS PERFECT.
THE POET NAILED TO THE
BONE OF THE WORLD
COMES IN THROUGH A DOOR,
TO LIVE UNTIL
HE DIES,
WHATEVER HAPPENS IN BETWEEN,
IN THE NIGHT OF THE LIVING
DEAD, THE POET REMAINS ALIVE,
    A FISH WITH FROG'S
    EYES,
    CREATION IS PERFECT.
THE POET WALKS ON THE EARTH
AND OBSERVES THE SILENT
SPHINX UPON THE NILE.
THE POET KNOWS HE MUST
WRITE THE TRUTH,
EVEN IF HE IS
KILLED FOR IT, FOR THE
SPHINX CANNOT BE DENIED.
WHENEVER A MAN DENIES IT,
A MAN DIES.
THE POET LIVES IN THE
MIDST OF DEATH
AND SEEKS THE MYSTERY OF
LIFE, A STONE REALITY IN THE

REALM OF SYMBOLS, FANTASY, AND
METAPHOR, FOR REASONS
THAT ARE HIS OWN WHAT IS REAL
IS THE PIT OF BONES HE COMES
FROM,

    A FISH WITH FROG'S
    EYES,
    CREATION IS PERFECT.
SOMEWHERE A BUDDHA SITS IN
SILENCE AND HOLDS THE
POET AND THE WORLD IN
SEPARATE HANDS AND REALIZES HE
IS BORN TO
DIE.
THE BLOOD OF THE POET
MUST FLOW IN HIS POEM,
SO MUCH SO, THAT OTHERS
DEMAND AN EXPLANATION.
THE POET ANSWERS THAT THE
POEM IS NOT TO BE
EXPLAINED. IT IS WHAT IT
IS, THE REALITY OF THE POEM
CANNOT BE DENIED,

    A FISH WITH FROG'S
    EYES,
    CREATION IS PERFECT.
THE POET IS ALONE WITH OTHERS
LIKE HIMSELF. THE PAIN IS BORN
INTO THE POET. HE MUST LIVE
WITH IT. IT IS HIS SOURCE OF
PURITY, SUFFERING HIS
LEGACY,
THE POET HAS TO BE A
STONE.

    A FISH WITH FROG'S
    EYES,
    CREATION IS PERFECT.

69

WHEN THE POET PROTESTS THE
DEATH HE SEES AROUND
HIM,
THE DEAD WANT HIM SILENCED.
HE DIES LIKE LORCA DID,
YET LORCA SURVIVES IN HIS
POEM, WOVEN INTO THE DEEPS
OF LIFE. THE POET SHOCKS THOSE
AROUND HIM. HE SPEAKS OPENLY
OF WHAT AUTHORITY HAS DEEMED
UNSPEAKABLE, HE BECOMES THE
ENEMY OF AUTHORITY. WHILE THE
POET LIVES, AUTHORITY
DIES. HIS POEM IS
FOREVER.
WHEN THE POET DIES,
A STONE IS PLACED ON
HIS GRAVE, IT IS HIM,
A PIT OF BONES,
    CREATION IS PERFECT,
IN THE PIT OF BONES
A SKY OF STARS, A HEAVEN OF
SUNS AND MOONS, AND THE GREAT
SUN IN THE CENTER,
    CREATION IS PERFECT.
A MASK CREATED IN THE PIT
IS THE IMAGE OF THE POET.
THE IMAGE OF THE POET
IS A
SECRET.
    A FISH WITH FROG'S
    EYES,
    CREATION IS PERFECT.
I HAVE WALKED IN THIS WORLD
WITH A CLOAK OF DEATH WRAPPED
AROUND ME. I WALKED ALONE, EVERY

KISS WAS A WOUND, EVERY SMILE
A THREAT.
ONE DAY DEATH REMOVED HIS
CAPE FROM AROUND ME,
I UNDERSTOOD WHAT I HAD LIVED
THROUGH. I HAD NO REGRETS,
WHEN THE CLOAK WAS REMOVED,
I WAS IN A PIT OF BONES,
    A FISH WITH FROG'S
    EYES,
    CREATION IS PERFECT.

LONE EAGLE

IT IS SARASWATI AGAIN,
IN THE DANCE OF SHIVA,
THE ONLY DANCE THERE IS,
VINCENT VAN GOGH'S CUT OFF
EAR FLOWING THROUGH THE
IMPRESSIONISTIC SKY, THE BEAUTIFUL
FACE OF RIMBAUD ILLUMINATES
THE FURY MICHELANGELO
HAS RELEASED UPON THE
WORLD. CHARLES LINDBERGH
DREAMS OF THE WATERS HE HAS SEEN.

I AM A CAMERA

THE POET NAILED ON
THE HARD BONE OF THIS WORLD,
HIS SOUL DEDICATED TO SILENCE
IS A FISH WITH FROG'S EYES,
THE BLOOD OF A POET FLOWS
OUT WITH HIS POEMS, BACK
TO THE PYRAMID OF BONES
FROM WHICH HE IS THRUST
HIS DEATH IS A SAVING GRACE

CREATION IS PERFECT

JANUARY 30, 1976: MESSAGE TO MYSELF

It is the time of illusion and reality,
Russia deliberately creates the illusion of
        wanting peace,
While preparing feverishly for war.
The slogans used by Communism are based on a desire
        for peace,
They are illusionary, for they are desiring an atmosphere
        for war.
The U.N. wants peace, but it must be careful
Not to compromise itself by settling for peace
At any cost. The West cannot rest easy, for Russia is
Anxious for war, while Russia cannot risk a unified
        Germany.
All the contradictions of the situation heighten the
Dangers of war.

The Ancient Rain is falling. It is falling on the
        N.A.T.O. meetings,
It is falling in Red Square. Will there be war or peace?
The Ancient Rain knows, but does not say.
I make speculations of my own, but I do not discuss them
Because the Ancient Rain is falling.

The Ancient Rain is falling all over America now.
The music of the Ancient Rain is heard everywhere.

THE ANCIENT RAIN

At the illusion world that has come into existence of world that exists secretly, as meanwhile the humorous Nazis on television will not be as laughable, but be replaced by silent and blank TV screens. At this time, the dead nations of Europe and Asia shall cast up the corpses from the graveyards they have become. But today the Ancient Rain falls, from the far sky. It will be white like the rain that fell on the day Abraham Lincoln died. It shall be red rain like the rain that fell when George Washington abolished monarchy. It shall be blue rain like the rain that fell when John Fitzgerald Kennedy died.

They will see the bleached skeletons that they have become. By then, it shall be too late for them. All the symbols shall return to the realm of the symbolic and reality become the meaning again. In the meantime, masks of life continue to cover the landscape. Now on the landscape of the death earth, the Luftwaffe continues to fly into Volkswagens through the asphalt skies of death.

It shall be black rain like the rain that fell on the day Martin Luther King died. It shall be the Ancient Rain that fell on the day Franklin Delano Roosevelt died. It shall be the Ancient Rain that fell when Nathan Hale died. It shall be the brown rain that fell on the day Crispus Attucks died. It shall be the Ancient Rain that fell on July Fourth, 1776, when America became alive. In America, the Ancient Rain is beginning to fall again. The Ancient Rain falls from a distant secret sky. It shall fall here on America, which alone, remains alive, on this earth of death. The Ancient Rain is supreme and is aware of all things that have ever happened. The Ancient Rain shall be brilliant yellow as it was on the day Custer died. The Ancient Rain is the source of all things, the Ancient Rain knows all secrets, the Ancient Rain illuminates America. The Ancient Rain shall kill genocide.

The Ancient Rain shall bring death to those who love and feel only themselves. The Ancient Rain is all colors, all forms, all shapes, all sizes. The Ancient Rain is a mystery known only to itself. The Ancient Rain filled the seas. The Ancient Rain killed all the dinosaurs and left one dinosaur skeleton to remind the world that the Ancient Rain is falling again.

The Ancient Rain splits nations that have died in the Ancient Rain, nations so that they can see the culture of the living dead they have become, the Ancient Rain is falling on America now. It shall kill D. W. Griffith and the Ku Klux Klan; Hollywood shall die in the Ancient Rain. This nation was born in the Ancient Rain, July 4, 1776. The Ancient Rain shall cause the Continental Congress to be born again.

The Ancient Rain is perfection. The Ancient Rain cured the plague without medicine. The Ancient Rain is vindictive. The Ancient drops are volcanoes and in one moment destroyed Pompeii and brought Caesar down, and now Caesar is fallen. This Roman Empire is no more. The Ancient Rain falls silently and secretly. The Ancient Rain leaves mysteries that remain, and no man can solve. Easter Island is a lonely place.

The Ancient Rain wets people with truth and they expose themselves to the Ancient Rain. Egypt has a silent sphinx and pyramids made of death chambers so that Egypt remembers the day the Ancient Rain drowned it forever. The mummies no longer speak, but they remember the fury of the Ancient Rain. Their tombs have been sawed in pieces and moved to the graveyard to make way for the pool of Ancient Rain that has taken their place.

The Ancient Rain saw Washington standing at Appomattox and it fell on Lee as he laid down his sword. The Ancient Rain fell on the Confederacy and it was no more.

The Ancient Rain is falling again. The Ancient Rain is falling on the waves of immigrants who fled their homelands to come to this home of Ancient Rain to be free of tyranny and hunger and injustice, and who now refuse to go to school with Crispus Attucks, the Ancient Rain knows they were starving in Europe. The Ancient Rain is falling. It is falling on the N.A.T.O. meetings. It is falling in Red Square. Will there be war or peace? The Ancient Rain knows, but does not say. I make speculations of my own, but I do not discuss them, because the Ancient Rain is falling.

The Ancient Rain is falling in the time of a war crisis, people of Europe profess to want peace, as they prepare day and night for war, with the exception of France and England. They are part of the N.A.T.O. alliance. I believe that Russia wants war. Russia supports any Communist nation to war with weapons and political stances on behalf of any Communist political move. This will eventually lead to war—a war that shall make World War Three, the largest war ever.

The Ancient Rain is falling all over America now. The music of the Ancient Rain is heard everywhere. The music is purely American, not European. It is the voice of the American Revolution. It shall play forever. The Ancient Rain is falling in Philadelphia. The bell is tolling. The South cannot hear it. The South hears the Ku Klux Klan, until the bell drowns them out. The Ancient Rain is falling.

The Ancient Rain does what it wants. It does not explain to anyone. The Ancient Rain fell on Hart Crane. He committed suicide in the Gulf of Mexico. Now the Washington Monument is bathed in the celestial lights of the Ancient Rain. The Ancient Rain is falling in America, and all the nations that gather on the East River to try to prevent a star prophecy of 37 million deaths in World War III. They cannot see the Ancient Rain, but live in it, hoping that it does not want war. They would be the

77

victims . . . in Asia, the Orient, Europe, and in South America. The Ancient Rain will cause them to speak the languages they brought with them. The Ancient Rain did not see them in America when Crispus Attucks was falling before the British guns on the Boston Commons. The Ancient Rain is falling again from the place where the Ancient Rain lives. Alone. The Ancient Rain thinks of Crockett and falls on the Santa Ana Freeway and it becomes a smog source.

The Ancient Rain wets my face and I am freed from hatreds of me that disguise themselves with racist bouquets. The Ancient Rain has moved me to another world, where the people stand still and the streets moved me to destination. I look down on the Earth and see myself wandering in the Ancient Rain, ecstatic, aware that the death I feel around me is in the hands of the Ancient Rain and those who plan death for me and dreams are known to the Ancient Rain . . . silent, humming raindrops of the Ancient Rain.

The Ancient Rain is falling. The Washington
    Monument rumbles.
The Lincoln Memorial is surrounded by stars.
Mount Rushmore stares into every face.
The Continental Congress meets in the home of
    the Ancient Rain.
Nathan Hale stands immaculate at the entrance
    to the Capitol.
Crispus Attucks is taken to school by Thomas
    Jefferson.
Boston is quiet.
The Ancient Rain is falling.

The Ancient Rain is falling everywhere, in Hollywood, only Shirley Temple understands the Ancient Rain and goes to Ghana, Africa, to be ambassador. The Ancient Rain lights up Shirley Temple in the California sky. Meanwhile, in Atlanta, the German U.N. delegation sits comfortably eating in a restaurant that Negro soldiers can't get into, as of some deal between the Germans and the Ku Klux Klan.

The Ancient Rain is falling on the restaurant. The Southern bloc cannot see it.

The Ancient Rain is falling on the intellectuals of America. It illuminates Lorca, the mystery of America shines in the Poet in New York. The Negroes have gone home with Lorca to the heaven of the lady whose train overflows. Heaven.

The Negroes have gone home to be enclosed by the skirts of their little girl mother. Black angels roam the streets of the earth. Make no mistake, they are angels, each angel is Abraham Lincoln, each angel is guarded by Ulysses S. Grant. They are for the death of the Ku Klux Klan at Appomattox. The sword of Lee is no more.

The Daughters of the Confederacy are having a luncheon at the Beverly Hills Hotel in the Savoy room. They are not Daughters of the American Revolution. They are not the Mothers of Crispus Attucks. They shall have Baked Alaska for dessert. Their lunch is supervised by a Japanese steward, the French caterer has provided them with special gray napkins.

The voice of Robert E. Lee cannot be heard over the rumbles of Grant's tomb. They leave as they came, the Daughters of the Confederacy, each enclosed in her own Appomattox. Back home they go to Cockalo. Crispus Attucks lying dead on the Boston Commons is the burning of Atlanta by the Union Army. John Brown was God's Angry Man. Crispus Attucks is the black angel of America. Crispus Attucks died first for the American Revolution, on the opening day of American glory. Crispus Attucks does not want a white mother. Crispus Attucks is the Blackstone of the American Revolution that is known to

God. Crispus Attucks is not the son of the South, not the son of Lee, not the son of Jefferson Davis. The South cannot have Attucks for a son. Crispus Attucks is my son, my father, my brother, I am Black.

Crispus Attucks will never fight for Russia. That cannot be said of the Rosenbergs or Alger Hiss or Whittaker Chambers. Crispus Attucks lives in heaven with Nathan Hale. They go to the same school. They do not live in the South.

I see the death some cannot see, because I am a poet spread-eagled on this bone of the world. A war is coming, in many forms. It shall take place. The South must hear Lincoln at Gettysburg, the South shall be forced to admit that we have endured. The black son of the American Revolution is not the son of the South. Crispus Attucks' death does not make him the Black son of the South. So be it. Let the voice out of the whirlwind speak:

> Federico García Lorca wrote:
> Black Man, Black Man, Black Man
> For the mole and the water jet
> Stay out of the cleft.
> Seek out the great sun
> Of the center.
> The great sun gliding
> over dryads.
> The sun that undoes
> all the numbers,
> Yet never
> crossed over a
> dream.

The great sun gliding over dryads, the sun that undoes all the numbers, yet crossed over a dream. At once I am there at the great sun, feeling the great sun of the center. Hearing the Lorca music in the endless solitude of crackling blueness. I could feel myself a little boy again in crackling blueness, wanting to do what Lorca says in crackling blueness to kiss out my frenzy on bicycle wheels and smash little squares in the flush of a soiled exultation. Federico García Lorca sky, immaculate scoured sky, equaling only itself contained all the distances that Lorca is, that he came from Spain of the Inquisition is no surprise. His poem of solitude walking around Columbia. My first day in crackling blueness, I walked off my ship and rode the subway to Manhattan to visit Grant's tomb and I thought because Lorca said he would let his hair grow long someday crackling blueness would cause my hair to grow long. I decided to move deeper into crackling blueness. When Franco's civil guard killed, from that moment on, I would move deeper in crackling blueness. I kept my secrets. I observed those who read him who were not Negroes and listened to all their misinterpretation of him. I thought of those who had been around him, those that were not Negro and were not in crackling blueness, those that couldn't see his wooden south wind, a tiltin' black slime that tacked down all the boat wrecks, while Saturn delayed all the trains.

I remember the day I went into crackling blueness. His indescribable voice saying Black Man, Black Man, for the mole and the water jet, stay out of the cleft, seek out the great Sun of the Center.

INDEX OF TITLES AND FIRST LINES

84